Praise for *1-2-3 Magic for Kids*

"If you have children, **you must have this book!** It is so
easy for kids to read and really makes an impression on
how they can participate in a happy, healthy home."

"**We have tried EVERYTHING** for our very strong-willed
daughter! Started reading this and it was **the first thing to work!**"

"*1-2-3 Magic for Kids* is **highly recommended** for
all parents who are unsure of what to do or what
to say when their children fail to listen."

"**This book is wonderful** for helping parents explain
the new 'rules' to children. It is told in a storybook
fashion that **children can easily relate to**."

"This book is **great to read to your children** to
help them understand the new parenting style."

"**My child was excited about this
program** after reading this book."

What parents are saying about *1-2-3 Magic*:

"This book **changed our lives**."

"My three-year-old has become a different little girl, **and she is so much happier now**."

"**The ideas in this book work!** It really is like magic! I feel like **I am back in charge**."

"Simple, clear, concise, and **easy to follow**."

"**I highly recommend this book** if you need a method of dealing with your little one(s) that keeps everyone calm."

"Extremely **helpful and informative**."

"A **great book** for any parent!"

"**I was desperate for a change** in my family dynamics. **This book was the answer!**"

"**Fantastic book** that really helps with toddler tantrums. **My husband and I both read it** and now **we are disciplining in the same way**. This book has been a **life saver!**"

"*1-2-3 Magic* **simplifies everything** I've read in other books, which makes it **very easy to follow**. Our home has become **a much more positive place**."

"**Easy to read** and easy to follow."

"**Buy this book; read this book; follow the instructions in this book!** I highly recommend this to anyone involved in disciplining children."

"*1-2-3 Magic* **made parenting fun again**."

"All I have to say is that **the ideas in this book WORK!** It really is like magic!"

"**This book is amazing!** My three-year-old was having major tantrums 4–6 times a day, screaming at the top of his lungs. After applying *1-2-3 Magic*, he rarely has meltdowns."

"*1-2-3 Magic* **takes the stress out of discipline**."

"**It's such a relief to not feel like I'm constantly yelling at someone!** If you want to see a fast improvement in your child's behavior, check out *1-2-3 Magic*."

1·2·3
MAGIC
FOR KIDS

Helping Your Kids
Understand the New Rules

THOMAS W. PHELAN, PHD
AND TRACY M. LEE

Originally published in 2008 by ParentMagic, Inc. and distributed by Independent Publishers Group.

Published by Sourcebooks, Inc.
P.O. Box 4410, Naperville, Illinois 60567-4410
(630) 961-3900
Fax: (630) 961-2168
sourcebooks.com

Source of Production: Printplus Limited, Shenzhen, Guangdong Province, China
Date of Production: October 2020
Run Number: 5020005

Printed and bound in China.
PP 10 9

TABLE OF CONTENTS

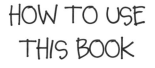

HOW TO USE THIS BOOK

1-2-3 Magic for Kids is designed to help parents explain America's simplest discipline program, *1-2-3 Magic: Effective Discipline for Children 2–12*, to their children. The parent version of the *1-2-3 Magic* book has sold more than 1.8 million copies because it's easy to learn, and it works.

Most books about child discipline explain the program to the parents. The parents then explain the program to the kids. *1-2-3 Magic for Kids*, however, explains the new discipline methods directly to the children (with parents' help for younger kids). The book is presented from the point of view of young children and includes games, puzzles, questions for discussion, and 4-color illustrations.

If you are about to start using 1-2-3 Magic with your youngsters, *1-2-3 Magic for Kids* will be a valuable tool in explaining to your children exactly what 1-2-3 Magic is and how it works. If you are already using 1-2-3 Magic with your children, *1-2-3 Magic for Kids* will help reinforce and refresh what your kids already know about the program.

If your kids are prereaders, start by reading **Part I: The Story of Rachel and Maddie**, with your children. Allow them to interrupt, ask questions, or read sections themselves, as you would with any story. The story is simple and short, so many preschoolers can sit through the whole thing.

If your kids are more advanced readers, have them read the story themselves or read it to you. The kids may then want to ask you questions, or you can ask them questions about what they read.

Once the children know the Story of Rachel and Maddie, the other chapters will be easy to understand. If the kids want, they can read straight through chapters 6–9 (alone or with you), or they can check out each chapter one at a time. The order of the chapters is not critical.

Chapter 6: The 1-2-3 Magic Tool Kit explains the various strategies moms and dads will use to reinforce good behavior, control difficult behavior, and strengthen their relationships with their children, such as counting, praise, and one-on-one fun. Chapter 6 will also reinforce parents' knowledge of what they need to be doing!

Chapter 7: Kids' Questions about 1-2-3 Magic lists the things youngsters most commonly inquire about before starting the program. After reading the Story of Rachel and Maddie, your children will probably come up with a few of these questions on their own.

Chapter 8: Fun Activities and Puzzles includes some simple exercises that highlight 1-2-3 Magic concepts. Activities that may require a little parental assistance are marked with this:

Chapter 9: What Will Our Family Be Like Afterward?
will help children understand why their parents are starting 1–2–3
Magic in the first place. The easiest of all the chapters, chapter
9 shows simple scenes involving improved behavior, better
relationships, and a happier, less-stressful family life as a result of
1–2–3 Magic.

1-2-3 Magic for Kids contains elements of fiction, nonfiction,
and hands-on learning activities. This book will appeal to children
in different age groups and with various learning styles so that
the widest variety of children will benefit from the information
provided. Most importantly, *1-2-3 Magic for Kids* will help parents
and kids enjoy one another's company.

Hello. I'm Ben, and I'm eight years old.

I'm here to tell you about why this book, 1-2-3 Magic for Kids, was written. A few years ago, my family moved to a new town because of my dad's job. It was hard for all of us. I couldn't stand my new teacher, my sister was sad because of leaving her friends, and my parents were arguing a lot. My sister and I fought more than ever (of course, it was almost always her fault). I used to pretend that I was sick so that I didn't have to go to school in the mornings, and my sister whined and yelled all the time. Before the move, being at home with my family used to be fun, but after the move, it just plain stunk! No one was happy, and we all just tried to stay out of each others' way.

Finally, my parents decided that we all needed some help getting used to our new life in this new town. We went to this lady called a "psychologist." She taught my parents the 1-2-3 Magic program. Basically, it's a program that helps parents get kids to behave—without yelling or spanking. It's a good thing, but when my sister and I first found out about it, we weren't happy at all. Mom and Dad explained it to us, though, and once we got going, we found out that it was pretty cool. My parents helped us to stop doing what we needed to stop (like arguing) and to start doing what we needed to start (like getting ready for school)! They stopped yelling so much, and then we stopped yelling too. It was really kind of a relief.

Well, here's where this book comes in. When my parents started using 1-2-3 Magic, they had a book and a couple of DVDs that taught them what to do. My sister and I wanted to see them too, but they were too hard for us to understand. It was too much grown-up stuff. So this book is just for kids! It explains 1-2-3 Magic in a way that makes sense to us. There's a cool story in here and some games too!

Now my parents have their book, and we have ours! And we have a home again where everyone is happy most of the time. That's the best part. Well, enjoy this book, and I'll check in with you now and then!

Part 1

The Story of Rachel and Maddie

Chapter 1

WHAT IS 1-2-3 MAGIC?

This is the story of two kids named Maddie and Rachel. Rachel's parents are divorced, and they both use 1-2-3 Magic with her and her brother, Marc. Maddie and her parents yell at each other all the time. Maddie won't do what she's supposed to, and her parents get mad. In the story, Rachel helps Maddie understand what 1-2-3 Magic is and how it's helped her family to be a lot happier and have more fun together.

Rachel was in her backyard, sliding down the sliding board on her swing set. She loved to slide! Her best friend, Maddie, who lived right next door, loved to slide too. The girls liked it when their mothers took them to the park around the corner because there was the longest, most slippery slide in the world right in their own neighborhood.

Rachel and Maddie had lived next door to each other since they were little babies. In fact, Rachel couldn't remember a time when Maddie's family wasn't right on the other side of her backyard fence! Rachel and Maddie were in second grade together. They both loved their teacher and were so happy to be in the same class!

Even when they weren't in school, the two girls were always together. They loved to ride their bikes, play games, and have sleepovers. Sleepovers were their favorite! They usually stayed at Rachel's house when they spent the night together because Maddie's mom and dad yelled an awful lot. It made Rachel's tummy hurt when that happened. Maddie's parents were nice people, but she didn't like screaming at all. It reminded her of her own mom before she started using 1-2-3 Magic.

What is 1-2-3 Magic? 1-2-3 Magic is a way for your parents to help you stop doing "bad" things and start doing "good" things without yelling or spanking.

One day, as Rachel was playing on the slide in her backyard, she could hear yelling through the open windows at Maddie's house. She didn't know what was going on.

First, she heard Maddie yelling and then her mom yelling. Then Maddie was yelling LOUDER, and then her mom was yelling even LOUDER THAN THAT! Suddenly, their back door flew open, and Maddie came running out into her backyard. She was crying really, really hard. Rachel wondered why Maddie was so upset. She jumped over the fence between their houses quickly to get to her friend.

"What's wrong, Maddie?" asked Rachel.

"My mom is so mean!" wailed Maddie.

"What did she do?" Rachel asked.

Maddie said, "She told me that I had to clean my room before we could go to my grandma's this afternoon. It's Saturday morning! I don't *want* to clean my room! She said that our weekend was going to be busy, so I had to do it right now! I yelled that I was NOT going to do it and went in my room and slammed the door. Then, Mommy came in and started screaming at me that I had better clean my room, or I'd be in really big trouble."

"Telling you to clean up your room isn't that mean," Rachel said.

"No, I guess that wasn't so mean. The mean part was when she yelled at me," said Maddie. Her face looked so sad.

"Didn't you yell at her first?" Rachel asked.

"I don't care. She's still MEAN!" Maddie argued.

"Yeah, I don't like to be yelled at either. My mom used to yell all the time before we started 1-2-3 Magic," said Rachel.

"1-2-3 Magic? What's that?" Maddie asked.

"1-2-3 Magic is a nice way for parents to get kids to behave. We've been doing it at our house for a long time. I really like it. I didn't at first, but now everyone in my family is a whole lot nicer. I'm really glad that my mom and dad both use it!" Rachel said.

"Does your mom know magic?" Maddie asked.

"Well, it's not *really* magic. It's just called magic. I don't really know why," replied Rachel.

"Maybe it's called 'magic' because it magically keeps your mom from yelling and getting so mad all the time!" said Maddie.

Excitedly, Rachel said, "Hey, I bet that's it!"

The best thing about 1-2-3 Magic is that there is no more yelling and no more spanking!

Chapter 2

WHAT IS COUNTING?

Maddie's house in this story reminds me of what my house used to be like. All that arguing and yelling was a big pain.

"Why don't we go inside and clean your room together?
Then we can go to my house to play," said Rachel.

"You'll help me?" asked Maddie.

"Sure. If we do it together, we'll get done really fast!"
Rachel said, as she went running toward Maddie's house.

Rachel was putting away a box of puzzle pieces that had fallen on the floor, and Maddie was picking up her dirty clothes to put in her hamper. Maddie started thinking about what Rachel had told her about this "1-2-3" thing.

"Hey, Rachel...how does that whole 1-2-3 Magic thing work?" asked Maddie.

"Well, whenever I start to do something that I shouldn't do, like tease my brother, Mom says, 'That's 1.' If I stop doing it, nothing happens. If I don't stop, she says, 'That's 2.' That's my last chance to stop it. If I *still* don't stop, she says 'That's 3, take 7,'" Rachel explained.

"What does 'take 7' mean?" Maddie looked confused.

"That means that I have to go to my room for 7 minutes," Rachel said.

"7 is kind of a weird number," said Maddie.

"I have to go for 7 minutes because I'm 7 years old. If I were 5 years old, I would have to go for 5 minutes. Get it?" asked Rachel.

"Oh, yeah, I see!" Maddie understood it now.

"That's called 'counting.' In 1-2-3 Magic, that's what parents do to make you stop doing things that they don't want you to do," Rachel told her.

WHY DO THEY COUNT TO 3?

Your parents want to teach you to do the right thing. They give you the "1" and the "2" to give you a chance to figure out how to do the right thing all by yourself!

The girls had finished cleaning Maddie's room. It really did go faster when two people cleaned up together! They decided to go over to Rachel's house to play with their dolls.

Maddie grabbed her favorite doll from her bed, and they took off!

The girls were in Rachel's living room giving their baby dolls bottles. Maddie said, "You know what? Sometimes when my parents tell me to go to my room, I tell them 'No!' Do you ever do that?"

"Sometimes when I'm really mad I say that," Rachel answered. "Then my mom gives me another choice."

"I don't get it," said Maddie. "All you have to do is say 'no,' and then you don't have to go to your room?" Maddie was completely amazed!

Rachel said, "Well, it's not exactly like that. If I won't go to my room for 7 minutes after she counts to 3, she either takes money from my allowance or makes me go to bed really early or something. Then she lets me choose. I almost always decide that I'd rather go to my room. The other choice is usually *way* worse than 7 minutes in my own room!" Rachel told her.

"Yeah, 7 minutes in your room isn't that bad. Can you play while you're in there?" Maddie asked her friend.

"I can play anything except video games. I can't watch television, either. The best part is that when my 7 minutes are over and I leave my room, my mom is nice to me again. She doesn't yell at me or tell me that I was bad. We just act like nothing ever happened!" Rachel explained.

Maddie asked, "So all she does is count? She doesn't yell?"

"Nope, not anymore!" Rachel said.

"Wow! So that's why it's always so much quieter over here at your house!" Maddie had finally figured it out. She had always wondered about that.

"Let's go get a snack!" Rachel said.

Counting helps us to remember that Mom and Dad are in charge!

Chapter 3

HOW WILL THEY GET ME TO CLEAN MY ROOM?

How do you think Maddie feels about 1-2-3 Magic so far? I don't think she knows yet. She needs Rachel to tell her more about it.

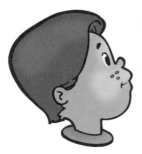

The following afternoon, Maddie was back at Rachel's house again. The girls were sitting in the kitchen eating some milk and cookies that Rachel's mom had made for them.

"You know," said Maddie, "that counting thing wouldn't have worked at my house yesterday. I wasn't doing anything bad. My mom didn't want me to stop doing something. She wanted me to start cleaning my room."

"Well, 1-2-3 Magic is not just for when you're doing bad stuff," replied Rachel. "It's also to help you do good things."

"So what do your mom and dad do to get you to do good things?" Maddie wanted to know.

"Well," started Rachel, "one thing is, if my mom had wanted me to clean my room this morning, and I wouldn't do it, she would have done it for me."

"WHAT?!" Maddie interrupted. "She would have just DONE it for you?!"

"Wait a minute! I'm not finished! She would have done it for me, but then she would have docked my allowance," finished Rachel.

"Docked? What does that mean?" asked Maddie.

"It means that my mom would have cleaned my room for me, but I would have to pay her for it out of my allowance," Rachel replied.

"Does she get mad when she has to do it for you?" asked Maddie.

"No, she doesn't get mad at all because she's getting my money! That doesn't happen very often, though. I'd rather clean my own room and keep my money, so now I just go ahead and do it when she tells me to," Rachel said.

"Yeah, I wouldn't want to have to give back my allowance, either," Maddie said. "What other kinds of things do your parents do?" Maddie thought this was really neat.

"Well, my brother, Marc, never wants to eat his dinner, so he used to just sit at the table and look at it all night. He's really picky, so he just wanted to skip dinner and get his dessert! My dad started using a kitchen timer while he ate. Do you know what that is?" Rachel asked Maddie.

"Isn't that one of those little clocks that you set, and it 'dings' after a few minutes?" Maddie asked.

"Yep! My dad sets the timer for 20 minutes. If Marc finishes his dinner before the timer goes off, he gets dessert. If he doesn't finish in time, no dessert," Rachel said.

"I bet he eats faster now!" Maddie smiled.

Rachel giggled. "He does! Now, he finishes before anyone else!"

"Sometimes," Rachel said, "my parents use charts. Those are really cool!"

"Charts?" asked Maddie.

"Yep! Before, I never wanted to get up in the mornings to get ready for school. Then, my mom made this really neat chart that had stuff on it like 'brush my teeth' and 'get dressed' and 'eat my breakfast.' Every morning, I get a sticker for each one of those things that I do when I'm supposed to. I can't complain about doing them, either. If I do, I don't get my sticker. When I earn enough of them, Mom lets me go to the store and buy a new book that I want. I *really* like charts!" Rachel exclaimed.

"All of this stuff sounds really neat," Maddie said.

"It is!" said Rachel. "You know what I really like, though? I like it when I do a good job on something, like getting ready for bed on time. Then, my parents tell me how proud they are that I did it all on my own, without them having to tell me. I feel happy when they say things like that, and then I'm proud of me too! That makes me want to keep doing those things!"

Maddie said, "I love it when my parents tell me that they're proud of me. Except it seems like they spend way more time telling me what I'm doing wrong." Maddie looked sad again, and Rachel felt sorry for her friend.

Maddie finished her cookies. "Well, I guess I need to go do my homework. Can you play outside tomorrow?"

"Yep," replied Rachel. "I'll see you then!"

WAYS PARENTS CAN HELP YOU DO THE THINGS THAT YOU'RE SUPPOSED TO DO:

- docking your allowance
- kitchen timers
- charts
- telling you that you're doing a good job

Chapter 4

IS IT REALLY THAT EASY?

When my parents started using 1-2-3 Magic, I wasn't sure what to think. Some things I liked, and some things I didn't. It took some getting used to.

Maddie and Rachel went back outside to play on Rachel's swing set. Maddie said, "So, I guess you were really happy when your parents started to use 1-2-3 Magic?"

Rachel's mother, Ms. Alvarez, had walked outside to see the girls and heard what Maddie said. "No way!" she laughed. "At first, Rachel and Marc were both REALLY upset about it!"

"They were?" asked Maddie, who was gliding on the swing. "Why?"

"At first, we didn't like that Mommy and Daddy were making us do a whole bunch of stuff that we didn't like. We didn't like going to our rooms when we did bad stuff. I still didn't want to get up for school or clean my room, and Marc didn't want to eat his dinner before he got his dessert," Rachel said.

Maddie looked at Rachel's mom. "How did you know that they didn't like it?"

"Well," Rachel's mom started, "they both started testing us quite a bit."

"What does 'testing' mean?" Maddie asked.

"That means that Rachel and Marc both started doing things to figure out whether we were really serious about using 1-2-3 Magic. Sometimes, Marc threw big temper tantrums! He would throw himself on the floor and start screaming and yelling when I had to count him for something. He would yell that I was mean and that he didn't like me anymore."

"What would you do then?" Maddie asked.

"I would count him for what he did wrong in the first place, and then I would count him again for the temper tantrum. After I counted him, I'd leave him alone. There isn't much of a reason to throw a great big fit if no one is around to watch it, is there?" Rachel's mom said.

Rachel and Maddie laughed. Maddie asked, "What else did Marc do?"

"Sometimes he would threaten to run away or to never speak to me again. When he used threats, I would do the same thing. I would count him for what he did wrong and count again for the threats! He learned very quickly that getting in trouble twice for the same thing was kind of silly."

"Hey, Mommy!" said Rachel. "I just thought of something! If Marc really decided never to speak to you again, that would mean that he wouldn't have any more temper tantrums! You can't scream at someone when you're not talking to them!"

"Wow, Rachel," her mom said. "I hadn't thought of that!" They all laughed.

Maddie asked, "What about Rachel? What did she do when she didn't get her way?"

Ms. Alvarez looked at Rachel on the swing and smiled. "Do you mind if I tell her, honey?"

Rachel looked a little embarrassed but said, "No, I guess not."

"Rachel used to badger me a lot," Ms. Alvarez said.

"What does that mean?" asked Maddie.

"Well, if she wanted to do something and I told her 'no,' she would follow me around saying 'pleeeease?' and 'but MOM!' over and over and over again. It really got on my nerves! I would count her for the badgering, and that stopped very quickly too."

"Other times," said Ms. Alvarez, "she would sit down and feel sorry for herself. She would get the saddest look!"

"I wanted to make you feel bad," Rachel muttered.

Ms. Alvarez smiled. "I know."

"Let me guess!" said Maddie. "You would count her for feeling sorry for herself!"

"Actually," said Ms. Alvarez, "I didn't count that. She wasn't really hurting anyone or throwing a fit. If she wanted to be sad and pout, I didn't like it, but that was up to her. She would get over it pretty quickly and then be right back to her normal, happy self!"

"Yeah… I guess you can't count kids for feeling bad. That wouldn't be very nice," Maddie replied.

"That's right, Maddie. It's OK to feel badly sometimes. As long as you don't try to make everyone else miserable too, you have every right to feel the way that you feel."

"So, is the 'testing' over now?" Maddie asked.

"Yep! For the most part, the testing is over. Once the kids found out that we were serious about 1-2-3 Magic, they didn't need to test us anymore."

"Hey, Mommy!" said Rachel, excitedly. "Will you take us to the park?"

"Sure! Maddie, run home and make sure that your mom and dad say that it's all right for you to go," answered Ms. Alvarez.

"OK! I'll be right back!" Maddie ran across Rachel's yard and jumped the fence to get to hers.

DIFFERENT KINDS OF TESTING ARE:

- temper
- threats
- badgering
- pouting
- buttering up
- physical tactics

Chapter 5

THE FUN STUFF!

Yeah, I threw a few fits too in the beginning. And sometimes I'd try to give my parents the "silent treatment." But then, you know what? I figured it was just easier to get along with everybody.

Maddie came back into Rachel's yard. She had brought her mom with her.

"Do you mind if I come along?" Mrs. Williams asked.

"We'd love for you to come!" replied Ms. Alvarez.

"Let's go!" shouted Rachel.

As they walked along, Maddie asked excitedly, "Hey, you guys! Will you tell my mom about 1-2-3 Magic?"

Rachel looked at Maddie's mom and said, "That's the way my parents get my brother and me to behave without yelling at us all the time."

"Well, that sounds like it really is magic!" Mrs. Williams said.

"No, it's not really magic. But it feels like it is, sometimes," laughed Rachel's mother.

"How does it work?" asked Maddie's mom.

"Well, when your kids do something that you want them to stop doing, like whining or arguing, you count to 3.

"The first two counts allow them the chance to straighten up on their own. If they get to 3, they're sent to time-out for a few minutes. The trick is that there is no yelling or spanking and not a lot of talking about what they did wrong. Most of the time, they know *exactly* what they did wrong without you having to say a word!"

"There are also tools in 1-2-3 Magic that help you to get your kids to do the things that you want them to do, like homework or getting up for school in the morning," Ms. Alvarez continued.

"That sounds really interesting…and it works?" asked Mrs. Williams.

Maddie yelled, "It really does, Mom! Can we do it?"

Ms. Alvarez laughed. "Well, there is a little more to it, of course. If you'd like to learn more about it, I have a book that you can borrow that explains the whole thing. It explains how to begin the program with a short Kickoff Conversation and then how to get down to business!"

"That would be great!" replied Mrs. Williams.

When they got to the park, Rachel and Maddie headed straight for the slide. Their mothers sat down on a bench to talk.

"You know," said Ms. Alvarez, "the best part about 1-2-3 Magic is how much more our family enjoys our time together than we used to."

"That sounds nice. It seems like all we ever do is fuss and argue at our house," replied Maddie's mom.

"That's how it used to be for us too. Now that we've put a stop to so much of the whining, arguing, and yelling, we can really listen to what our kids are saying. They know that as long as they're not screaming or whining at us, we will always try to help them find ways to fix whatever is bothering them. They also understand that they will follow the same rules in both of their homes."

"What happens when they do yell at you?" asked Mrs. Williams.

"We count them, and the yelling stops pretty quickly. After that, we can get back to talking about their problems and trying to find ways to solve them together."

Ms. Alvarez continued, "Another great thing about 1-2-3 Magic is now that we spend so much less time dealing with the kids' bad behavior, we have a lot more time to do fun things together! We play more games, read more books, and spend more time just hanging out! We don't have to do anything special. Just being together doing something simple like coloring a picture is a lot of fun."

Maddie ran over to the bench where her mother was sitting. "Are we gonna do it, Mom? Please, can we?"

Her mother smiled. "Yes, Maddie, I think we can try it. It sure sounds like something that would be good for our family, doesn't it?"

Rachel ran over to the bench too. "It's been great for us, hasn't it, Mommy?" she asked.

"It sure has!" she answered.

Maddie grabbed her mother's hand and yanked her off the bench. "C'mon Mom! Let's go swing together!"

Hand in hand, Maddie and her mother took off for the swings. When they got back from the park, Mrs. Williams borrowed the 1-2-3 Magic book from Rachel's house and read the whole thing. From that day on, Maddie and her parents began doing a lot less yelling and a whole lot more swinging!

⠀⠀Part 2⠀⠀

Important Things
about 1-2-3 Magic

Chapter 6

THE 1-2-3 MAGIC TOOL KIT

There are some big words in the 1-2-3 Magic book for grown-ups that are kind of hard for kids to understand. This chapter explains  them to you. That way, when you hear your mom and dad using them, you'll know what's going on!

Counting

Counting is what your mom and dad will do when you are doing something that you're not supposed to be doing, like teasing your brother or sister or throwing a great big fit when you don't get your way!

When you start misbehaving, they'll say, "That's 1." If you don't get your act together after about 5 seconds, they'll say, "That's 2." If you're being really stubborn and still won't straighten up, they'll wait about 5 more seconds and say, "That's 3, take 7" (if you're 7 years old). What's great about counting is that you get two whole chances to stop the bad behavior before anything happens. That's a pretty good deal!

Remember, you get one minute of time-out for every year of your age. So, how many minutes of time-out do you get if you're 8 years old? That's right! You get an 8-minute time-out.

CRYING WHINING
YELLING
POUTING STOMPING

That's One!

Praise

Praise is a word that means saying something to someone that makes him feel good about himself. Imagine that you look at the clock at 4:30 in the afternoon and think, "Wow! It's about time for me to start my homework." You go get your books, sit down at your desk, and get busy without anyone having to tell you to. Your dad sees you doing your homework and says, "I am so proud of you for starting your homework on your own! That's very responsible behavior! Great job!"

You're probably going to be glad that Dad noticed, and you'll be proud of yourself too! Being proud of yourself is such a great feeling that you'll want to keep doing things to bring that feeling back again and again!

GOOD JOB!

Simple Request

This could also be called "simple command." This is when your parents just tell you what they need you to do! For example, your mom says, "Your teeth need to be brushed within the next 15 minutes." If we do what we're told to do the first time we're told to do it, everyone is happy! Mom is happy because your teeth are clean, and you smell minty fresh.

You're happy because Mom isn't on your case about it every 5 minutes because it's already done!

Kitchen Timer

Have you ever seen a kitchen timer? It's a little clock with an arrow that you wind up, and it makes a noise—like a "ding"—when the arrow gets to zero. Timers can make very annoying chores fun. Yes, fun!

Let's say the phone rings, and it's Grandma telling your mom that's she's going to drop by in 15 minutes. Now Mom is in a panic! The house is a wreck! She needs the living room straightened up in a hurry, and it's clear by the way that she's running around in circles that she needs your help.

Someone gets the brilliant idea to set a timer for 10 minutes! You'll all race against the clock to see if you can clean up before it dings.

Tick, tock, tick, tock, the timer keeps saying. The last toy gets put away about 2 seconds before the timer dings! You did it! The house is clean (well, at least all the junk is thrown in a closet where Grandma can't see it!), and guess what? You discover that you actually had fun doing it!

Docking System

There is good news and bad news about the docking system. The good news is that this is a way to get your parents to do your chores for you with great big smiles on their faces. Well, there is a good reason that they're smiling—this is the bad news. They're smiling because you are paying them to do the work for you. Now you're thinking, "Oh, I knew there was a catch."

With the docking system, your parents give you the opportunity to get your own work done. They'll probably give you a time by which your work needs to be completed. If it's not done by that time, they won't nag you or yell at you (more good news!). They'll just do it for you and charge you a fee.

You'll probably find that they charge WAY more than you'd like to pay for their services. It's probably easier to just go ahead and do the work yourself.

By the way, they won't be using the docking system for homework! Teachers wouldn't like that one bit!

Natural Consequences

Natural consequences are those things that happen naturally, just like the name says. If you forget to take your lunch to school, you'll be hungry. If you go to bed too late, you'll be tired the next day. Sometimes, your parents will stay out of the way of your mistakes, and you'll have to face the consequences all on your own.

Some kids constantly complain about doing their homework and want their parents to quit nagging them about it. What if you were one of those kids, and one day, your parents stopped nagging you to do it? You might end up without your homework done the next day at school. Mom and Dad wouldn't write a note to the teacher to excuse you because, after all, it was your own fault, right? You're the one who didn't get the homework finished. You would have to go to school and accept whatever punishment the teacher handed out. That's a "natural consequence." If you make a bad decision, then you are the one who must pay the price for that decision.

Charting

There are some things that we have trouble doing without a little help from our parents. One example is getting up and out in the mornings. There are so many things that we have to do to get out the door that it can be very hard for us to organize it all in our brains! This is where charting can help.

Your mom or dad can make a chart for you listing all the things that you have to do to get ready in the mornings.

They'll list things like eating breakfast, getting dressed, brushing your teeth, and more. They may even list a time by which you have to have each thing completed. Then, they'll place a sticker, a check mark, or something similar next to every item that you completed on time. Maybe after you earn a certain number of these, you'll get a small prize. It could be a special outing with Mom or Dad, a small toy, staying up a little past your bedtime, or something else that you and your parents come up with together.

Hopefully, doing all of these things on time will become a habit, and then you won't need the chart anymore. You will have learned a new skill! When that happens, you'll feel really, really good about it. After that, you'll be ready to tackle something brand-new!

66

Counting (for Start Behaviors)

You thought that counting could only be used when your parents wanted you to stop doing something, didn't you? Actually, it can be used for a start behavior, something your parents want you to *start* doing, but only if the behavior is something that can be completed in 2 minutes or less. Here's an example.

Let's say that a girl named Abby comes home after school and drops her coat on the floor instead of hanging it in the closet where it belongs. Her dad needs her to pick up the coat and put it in the right place. This is a start behavior. It's something that he wants her to start doing. Hanging up a coat takes very little time. It can definitely be done in less than 2 minutes.

Her dad says, "Abby, please hang up your coat."

Abby says, "No."

Abby's dad says, "That's 1." He waits 5 seconds and says, "That's 2." Abby still stands there and stares at him. After 5 more seconds, her dad says, "That's 3, take 9," because Abby is 9 years old. Abby has to go to her room for 9 minutes because she wouldn't pick up her coat.

Counting won't be used for start behaviors like doing your homework. It takes a lot longer than 2 minutes to finish your homework, so your parents might choose another method like charting or praising you for doing a good job in order to help you with that kind of good behavior.

Encouraging Independence

This is a fancy term that means parents are letting kids learn how to do things by themselves. There are many times when parents need to step in and help out when you try to do something new. Some new things that we'd like to try (like cooking on a stove) can be dangerous if we don't have a parent around to help us out. Other things, though (like learning how to make ourselves a sandwich or learning how to wash the dishes), can be a little messy at first, but we have to try them so we can learn to do them well.

When your family is using 1-2-3 Magic, there will be times when you ask your parents if you can try something new, and they have to tell you no—either because it's dangerous, or it's just not a good time at the moment. There will be other times, though, when your parents will say, "Sure, you can!" Your parents want to help you grow up smart and strong, and they want you to be able to take care of yourself. Learning how to do that is going to be a lot of fun!

Affection and Praise

Affection is a word that means to show someone that you love them. Your parents can do this with a kiss on the cheek, a hug, or a pat on the back. There are many ways to show people that you love them. When people show us that they love us, it makes us feel warm and special inside. We enjoy feeling loved!

One of the reasons that families begin to use 1-2-3 Magic is because, sometimes, we spend too much time arguing and trying to get everyone to cooperate that there really isn't much time left over to show love to one another. After everyone gets used to 1-2-3 Magic, you'll find that the members of your family are in a much better mood a lot more often and have more time for the really important stuff like great big hugs!

Listening

This sounds really simple. We listen to people all the time! But there is a difference between hearing and listening. Listening means that we not only hear the words that other people say, but that we also try hard to understand what they are thinking and how they are feeling.

There is another part of 1-2-3 Magic that teaches parents how to really listen to what you have to say. Sometimes your mom and dad are busy. They're so busy that they hear your words, but they don't really understand how important your words are to you. It's not that they don't care. It's just that real listening takes practice.

Try telling your parents when you have a problem that you really need to talk about. If they can't take the time to give you their full attention right away, they'll tell you a time soon when they can. They might even be able to help you solve your problem. Even if they can't, though, you'll still know that they really listened to you and understand what you're going through. Sometimes, just knowing that someone is listening is enough to help you deal with a big problem all by yourself!

One-on-One Fun

One-on-one fun is really simple to understand. It means that one person is having fun with one other person. It's fun to do things as a family sometimes, but it's also a lot of fun to have your mom or dad all to yourself for a little while. Playing games, reading books, taking walks, or sharing a snack can be very special times that a parent shares with a child. If you have something that you need to talk to your mom or dad about, it's a lot easier to do it when no one else is around.

One-on-one fun time can often lead to conversations that you just can't have when the rest of your family is around.

It's important for every member of your family to have one-on-one fun time with every other member of your family. Even moms and dads need one-on-one fun time together. It helps everyone to feel close to everyone else. Besides that, just like the title of this page says, it's FUN!

Kickoff Conversation

This is when you and your parents sit down together to talk about starting 1-2-3 Magic. The Kickoff Conversation is very short—it only lasts about 5 or 10 minutes. Your mom and dad will just explain what 1-2-3 Magic is and how it works. In fact, this may even be the time that they choose to give you this book! They'll explain a little bit to you, and then you can go through this book with them or on your own. Everyone will be prepared for your new start!

Chapter 7

KIDS' QUESTIONS ABOUT 1-2-3 MAGIC

When parents start using 1-2-3 Magic, kids ask a lot of questions. You probably have some right now! Here are some of those questions, along with answers that are easy to understand.

Why would I want my parents to use 1-2-3 Magic?

The best thing about 1-2-3 Magic is that it will make your home much calmer and happier. You, your brothers, your sisters, and your parents will be angry a lot less often. 1-2-3 Magic lets your parents discipline much more quickly and gently, so they have more time to spend having fun with you!

What behaviors will be counted?

Your mom and dad will count behaviors that they want you to STOP. We've talked about these before. They're called "stop behaviors." Some examples of stop behaviors are whining, tantrums, arguing, teasing, fighting, and yelling. You can probably think of a few more behaviors that you could add to this list.

What if I won't
go to my room?

Your parents need your cooperation to get you to your room for your time-out. You need to use your own two legs to get up and get yourself there, right?

If you refuse to go to your room, your parents may decide to use what we call a "time-out alternative." Time-out alternatives are consequences that your mom or dad can use that don't require any help from you! They could deduct money from your allowance. They could take the television out of your room for a while. They could decide that you can't have a friend over that you had invited. The interesting thing about time-out alternatives is that they're almost always worse than spending a couple of minutes in your room. Most kids figure this out real quick!

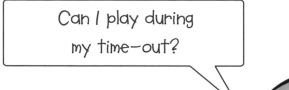

Can I play during
my time-out?

There are three things that aren't allowed during a time-out. First, you may not talk on the phone. Second, you may not have anyone in your room with you. Third, you may not use electronic equipment (TV, video games, computer, etc.). Other than that, you are allowed to entertain yourself. You can read, play with your toys, take a nap, or find something else to do.

What if I'm still mad and don't want to come out of my room when my time-out is over?

Stay in your room as long as you'd like. No one will bug you. Come out when you feel like it. (Wow, that was a really easy question!)

> Will I still be counted if I have a friend over?

Yep. If you're misbehaving with a friend over, you'll still be counted. If you get to 3, your friend will have to play alone for a bit while you're in your room. When you come out, you can explain to your friend what just happened. It won't take your friend long to get the whole counting thing!

> What happens if we're not at home?

If you aren't at home and you get to 3, your parents will do one of two things. They may find a time-out place wherever you happen to be. They could take you to the car, find a bench somewhere close by, or put really little kids in a shopping cart.

Another solution when you're out of the house is the time-out alternative that we talked about earlier. Your mom or dad may skip time-out altogether and decide to give you a different consequence, like an early bedtime or loss of a video game.

What happens if I'm fighting with my brothers or sisters, and I think it's their fault, and they think it's my fault?

Unless your mom or dad sees what happens or can VERY CLEARLY figure out who started the fight, both "fighters" will be counted. If the fight doesn't end, and you both get to 3, you'll both go to time-out. If you share a bedroom, you'll both be sent to different areas. If you're fighting to begin with, you probably won't want to be together anyway!

What happens if I don't do my chores?

There are a few things that parents can do to help you get your chores done. One is setting a kitchen timer. The timer helps you make your chores into a race and, believe it or not, can even make them fun sometimes! Your mom and dad can also try charting. Maybe you can even earn a small prize after a certain period of time, if you learn to do your chores on your own.

Believe it or not, your parents might even do your

chores for you—without even complaining about it! You're smiling right now, aren't you? Don't get too excited. You'll have to pay them to do your work for you. Parents tend to charge quite a bit of money if they have to do other people's work!

If we do charting, can I earn stuff?

Sometimes, your mom or dad may decide that you can earn a small prize if you do well on your chart. That is something that you will all decide together. Prizes are mainly to get you going, though, and they won't go on forever.

When can I say what I think?

You can say what you think to your parents anytime you want, as long as you're not yelling or attacking somebody. Your parents will try hard to be good listeners.

If you've just come out of a time-out, you may find your parents and CALMLY explain your side of things. Usually, there's no reason to do this, though, because it's mostly just the same old stuff. However, once your mom and dad decide that they have heard what you have to say and that the conversation is over, the discussion ends—whether you agree or not. If you continue talking and arguing, that's called "badgering," and you'll be counted all over again.

> What kinds of things can we do for one-on-one fun?

There are so many things that parents and kids can do for one-on-one fun! Here are just a few: play cards, read a book, play catch, go to a movie, go out for ice cream, do a puzzle, play hide-and-seek, or plant a small garden. We could go on and on! What could you add to this list?

> What if I live in two houses?

Families come in all different shapes and sizes. Some kids live in two homes. They split their time between Mom's house and Dad's house, or sometimes they live with a grandparent part of the time. Often, the adults in both homes decide to do 1-2-3 Magic together. That's wonderful, and it makes things a lot easier for you.

However, if only one grown-up in your life decides to follow the 1-2-3 program, that's still OK. Not everyone does everything the same way. That's especially true when it comes to helping kids to behave. It may be a good idea to talk about this a little more with the adult that is starting the 1-2-3 Magic program with you. He or she can help you figure out the best way to handle your own, unique situation!

Do you have any other questions about 1-2-3 Magic?

You may have other questions that we haven't covered here. That's great! Ask your mom and dad, and they'll do their best to answer your questions for you.

⫶⫶⫶ Part 3 ⫶⫶⫶
Things to Do and Things to Think About

Chapter 8

FUN ACTIVITIES AND PUZZLES

This chapter is full of cool stuff for you to do. There are puzzles, pictures to draw, and other things, too! They'll help you remember some of what you've learned in this book about 1-2-3 Magic. When you see this little hat  at the top of a page, that means you may need help from a grown-up.

🎓 Crossword Puzzle Start Behaviors

What are start behaviors? Start behaviors are those things that you do that your parents want you to START! Things like going to bed on time, doing your chores, and doing your homework are all start behaviors. The clues below all describe start behaviors. See if you can complete the crossword puzzle!

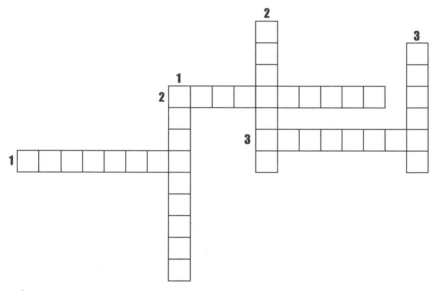

Across

1. Schoolwork that we do at home.
2. Playing a musical instrument at home.
3. When we sit down at the table and eat our food.

Down

1. Getting clothes and toys off the floor and back where they belong.
2. When we lay down at night to go to sleep.
3. Taking out the trash, washing dishes, and making beds.

What's Going to Happen Next?

Draw a picture of a temper tantrum.

What are stop behaviors? Stop behaviors are those things that you do that your parents want you to STOP! Things like fighting with your brother or sister or yelling when you're angry are examples of stop behaviors.

Crack the code! Below are blank spaces with numbers underneath them. Look at the table below and find the letter that represents each number. Place the right letter in each blank and you'll find a list of stop behaviors—in other words, behaviors that your parents would probably count.

1=A	2=B	3=C	4=D	5=E	6=F	7=G	8=H
9=I	10=J	11=K	12=L	13=M	14=N	15=O	16=P
17=Q	18=R	19=S	20=T	21=U	22=V	23=W	24=X
25=Y	26=Z						

___	___	___	___	___	___	___
1	18	7	21	9	14	7

___	___	___	___	___	___	___
20	5	1	19	9	14	7

___	___	___	___	___	___	___
23	8	9	14	9	14	7

___	___	___	___	___	___	___
25	5	12	12	9	14	7

___	___	___	___	___	___	___
16	15	21	20	9	14	7

___	___	___	___	___	___	___
20	1	14	20	18	21	13

Write about a time when you really wanted Mom or Dad to listen to you talk about something that was very important to you.

_____

_____

_____

_____

_____

_____

_____

_____

_____

_____

_____

_____

_____

_____

_____

How are the kids in the pictures feeling?

_____

_____

_____

_____

_____

_____

Draw a picture of you and your mom or dad having one-on-one fun!

🎓 True or False?

1. Going to bed is an example of a start behavior. T   F

2. Whining is an example of a start behavior. T   F

3. When kids are fighting, they should BOTH be counted most of the time. T   F

4. The Kickoff Conversation should take about 2 hours. T   F

5. If a child is acting up in public, a parent should quickly yell as loud as they can to get the kid's attention. T   F

6. With the docking system, Mom or Dad does the chore, and the child is sent to bed early. T   F

7. A timer should not be used for eating meals because it could upset someone's stomach. T   F

8. Listening and one-on-one fun are both ways to get along better with your parents. T   F

Answer Key

Crossword Puzzle: Answer to page 86

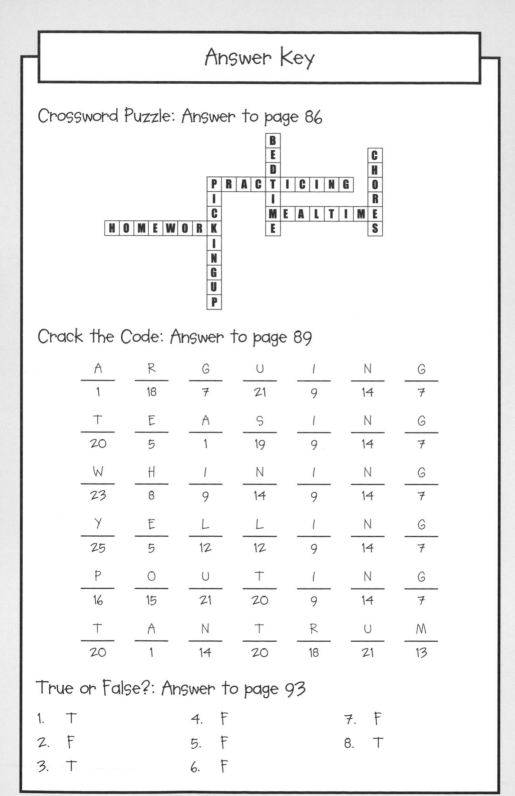

Crack the Code: Answer to page 89

A	R	G	U	I	N	G
1	18	7	21	9	14	7

T	E	A	S	I	N	G
20	5	1	19	9	14	7

W	H	I	N	I	N	G
23	8	9	14	9	14	7

Y	E	L	L	I	N	G
25	5	12	12	9	14	7

P	O	U	T	I	N	G
16	15	21	20	9	14	7

T	A	N	T	R	U	M
20	1	14	20	18	21	13

True or False?: Answer to page 93

1. T   4. F   7. F
2. F   5. F   8. T
3. T   6. F

94

Chapter 9

WHAT WILL OUR FAMILY BE LIKE AFTERWARD?

My life before 1-2-3 Magic was kind of miserable. After my parents started using it, though, things got a lot better! My whole family is happier now. Here are some of the things that you might notice in your own family after your mom and dad begin using 1-2-3 Magic.

98

Well, that's
1-2-3 Magic!

Hopefully, you understand it a lot better now. Pretty soon, your parents will get started. This is really going to make your family life so much happier.

1-2-3 Magic will help you learn how to do the things that you need to do. It will also help your parents to stay calm when you do something wrong. Living in a house where there is yelling all the time is no fun. It's no fun for your parents, and it's no fun for you! I know because I've been there! This program will help you get along much better with your parents and even your brothers and sisters. The best part is that you'll feel really great about yourself!

ABOUT THE AUTHORS

Photo courtesy of
Thomas W. Phelan,
PhD

Dr. Thomas W. Phelan is an internationally renowned expert, author, and lecturer on child discipline and attention-deficit/hyperactivity disorder. A registered PhD clinical psychologist, he appears frequently on radio and TV. Dr. Phelan practices and works in the western suburbs of Chicago.

Photo courtesy of
Tracy Lee

Tracy Lee is currently the family engagement specialist at the Virginia Department of Education. She has also been an elementary school teacher, preschool director, and the family resource coordinator for Colonial Heights Public Schools in Colonial Heights, Virginia. Additionally, she has appeared nationwide on ABC, CBS, NBC, and Fox affiliates, discussing parenting- and education-related issues.

IF YOU LOVED 1-2-3 MAGIC FOR KIDS...

check out these other products from
Thomas W. Phelan, PhD

1-2-3 Magic
Effective Discipline for Children 2–12

More 1-2-3 Magic DVD
Encouraging Good Behavior,
Independence, and Self-Esteem

Did You Know?
1-2-3 Magic, *1-2-3
Magic for Kids*, and the
1-2-3 Magic DVDs are
also available in
Spanish!

1-2-3 Magic Workbook
A user-friendly, illustrated companion to the *1-2-3 Magic* book that
includes case studies, self-evaluation questions, and exercises

1-2-3 Magic in the Classroom
Effective Discipline for Pre-K through Grade 8

1-2-3 Magic for Teachers DVD
Effective Classroom Discipline for Pre-K through Grade 8

1-2-3 Magic for Kids
Helping Your Children Understand the New Rules

1-2-3 Magic for Christian Parents
Effective Discipline for Children 2–12

1-2-3 Magic Starter Kit
Accessories to help you get started with the 1-2-3 Magic program

Tantrums! Book and DVD
Managing Meltdowns in Public and Private

Visit www.123magic.com